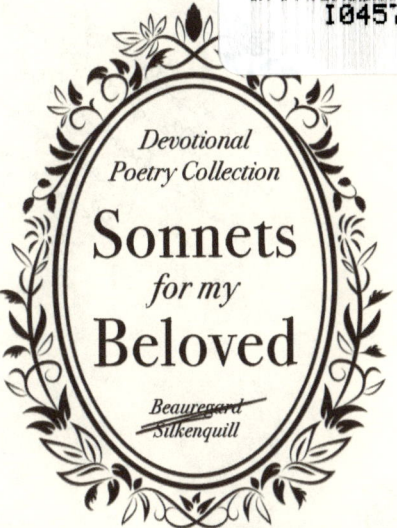

Devotional
Poetry Collection

Sonnets
for my
Beloved

~~Beauregard~~
~~Silkenquill~~

rewritten by
Mariselle Brightcrest
& Petunia Dawndale

with additional edits by
Evryn Rowanwood

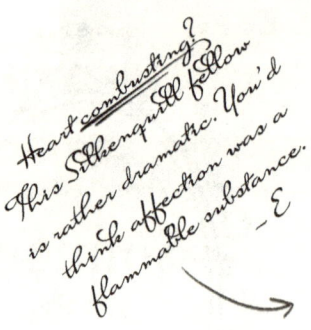

Heart combusting?
This Silkenquill fellow
is rather dramatic. You'd
think affection was a
flammable substance.
— E

Sonnets for my Beloved
by Beauregard Silkenquill

Based on characters and poems from the book *Deals & Dreams Spells* by Rachel Morgan.

Copyright © 2025 Rachel Morgan

ISBN 978-1-998988-35-8

Lord Evryn Rowanwood

To She Who Must Remain Nameless,
lest my heart combust upon the page

Brace yourself, Rowanwood.
The beauty of what you are about
to read is, I fear, terminal. – M

Tragic, really. The world
loses so many fine
gentlemen to poetry. – P

Do convey my dying wish:
that you never write poetry
EVER AGAIN.

not for long

Your golden hair, a cascade of light,
sets ~~my poer~~ heart afire at night.
~~I dream of braiding it into a rope,~~
~~and swinging from it, shrieking with~~ Hope.

I dream of strangling
myself with it after being
forced to recite this
abomination of a book.
— E

At least you'll die
surrounded by art. — P

Is that what we're calling this??

RUDE — M

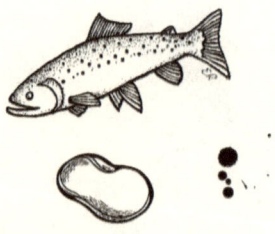

My darling muse, you radiant bean,
the brightest sprout I've ever seen.
Your smile, a sunrise on a trout,
I gasp, I flounder, I fall about.

Curious imagery. The juxtaposition of legumes and aquatic life suggests a poet untroubled by the constraints of habitat. - P

Indeed. A daring blend of agricultural and aquatic motifs. - M

this is truly awful

Is this supposed to be Cobalt??
Really, Rowanwood. If he were to
see this, he'd toss his mane in
horror and demand significantly
broader shoulders. – M

I don't believe I
asked for your
opinion.

logic clearly has absolutely nothing to do with this

```
Oh dearest heart, my sugared ham,
my golden goose, my velvet clam.
No poet's pen could ever convey
the way your glance makes logic sway.
```

Truly inspired. "Velvet clam" may well redefine the boundaries of romantic expression.

- P

Thank you. ♡

No. No no no no no.

- E

This "poetry" will be the death of me. – E

A tragedy of art — slain by beauty. – P

```
I ache, I yearn, I hum and whine,
each time I see your nose so fine.
I'd write an ode, I'd build a shrine,
but sneezed and lost the opening line.
```

What is this, Rowanwood?? – P

Me. Tearing my hair out over how absolutely TERRIBLE these verses are.

I see the resemblance. Though he has better hair than you. – M

Here's a poem for you:

My enchanted toadstool, muse of despair,
Your verses linger—everywhere.
They haunt the halls, they stain the air,
And rhyme with things that shouldn't dare.

My precious sapdrop, scourge of sense,
Each poem's worse than the last offense.
I read, I reel, I lose the will—
Your slam hants the page; stars help me, still.

O luminous pestilence, cease your art—
You've slain the English language's heart.
Should inspiration strike anew,
I beg—let it strike someone else, not you.

Such passion, Rowanwood.
- M

My beloved pumpkin paste,
your radiant face
makes my heart race
at frantic pace,
I fall, undone, in sweet disgrace.

I knew you had a poet's soul, Petunia. How modest of you to hide it all these years. ♥

I see now why she hid it.

So rude. No appreciation for true art. – P

this is true art →

(snort) It is not.

You simply could not bear it, could you...? The heat, the feeling, the glorious tubers of love—you had to prune them into submission. Tell me, Powanwood, do you fear passion, or only mine...?

O moderately attractive inhabitant
    of indeterminate terrain   beyond
O ~~fair one of the fertile plain,~~   repair
your love has ploughed my heart ~~again.~~
I till my soul, I ~~stoke the fire,~~
No ~~rutabaga of passion, turnip of desire~~!
Your ~~eyes like fire! Your~~ lips, a plum!
My reason's gone, my brain is numb.
On this point, the evidence is overwhelming.

        I attempt emotional gardening
            with limited success.

Your eyes are quite sufficient
    without combustion.

You've gutted it, Rowanwood.
Torn the passion straight from the soil. – P

iridescent menace
moon-kissed radish
enchanted compost heap
honey-soaked calamity
sweet hurricane
gilded crumpet of chaos

What is this?? - M

None of your business.

Are you brainstorming a list of the sweetest
pet names for our lovely Mari? - P

I would like to politely request
that the two of you stop stealing
this book and leaving additional
comments. You gifted it to ME,
did you not?

I burn like toast when you glance my way,
crisped by the heat of your gaze's ray.
The scent of longing fills the air,
a hint of smoke, of scorched affair.

this is actually
sweet, Rowanwood — M

He ... thank you? — E

much better than your deranged
hair-pulling self-portrait

I call it ...
"no goat theatrics required."

STARS, ROWANWOOD.
Are you saying the goat is ME??

No further comment

*Have I driven you
insane yet, Rowanwood?*

O cruel delight, O gentle pain,
your beauty drives me near insane
No soothing calm, no restful shroud —
each heartbeat croons your name aloud,
like a lovesick goat bleating
                              far too proud.

*I find myself beyond words.
The goat has taken them all.*

High praise. — P

That was not a compliment.

Your elbow, love, a work of art,
it bent and pierced my very heart.
No joint on earth could so beguile,
It beckoned me from half a mile.
It bends! It glints! It holds such style!
I faint! I swoon! I writhe awhile!

This may be my best work yet. — M

*Indeed. History shall mark this as
the day literature peaked. — P*

*I was present for its fall
immediately after.*

My Darling,

While organizing my study this afternoon,
this delightful specimen of 'literature'
tumbled from between two actually readable
volumes, and I was struck by a brilliant
notion. You mentioned earlier — between
your mother's third reminder about place
cards and your fourth cup of that
duskmint-vanilla tea you've become so
fond of — that you've yet to secure your
'something blue' for the ceremony.

Now, I realize your mother remains deeply
opposed to my brilliant suggestion of
returning your hair to that fetching azure
shade (a masterpiece of enchantment, if I
may say so myself). But observe, my darling
muse: the binding of this poetic atrocity
you so thoughtfully cursed upon me happens
to be … blue!

It's small enough to tuck into your bouquet,
though I confess I'd prefer you kept it
somewhere more … discoverable. Perhaps
aomehow hidden within the folds of your gown,
where we might unearth it together once all
the pageantry has concluded?

I imagine us, exhausted from the day's
proceedings, finding this ridiculous little
book and laughing — truly laughing — at the
wonderful absurdity of it all. At this
entire preposterous charade that somehow,
impossibly, led me to the realization that
the person I was meant to despise has become
the one I cannot imagine living without.

So yes, my blushberry bonbon, I propose
this collection of magnificently awful
poetry serve as your 'something blue'. It
seems fitting that an object originally
meant to embarrass me should instead become
a symbol of my complete and utter surrender
to the undeniable truth that _I love you_ —
genuinely, wholly, and with none of the
restraint that proper society would recommend.

Yours forever,
Evryn

Based on characters and poems from the book
Deals & Dreams Spells, part of The Charmed
Leaf Legacy series, by Rachel Morgan.

www.ingramcontent.com/pod-product-compliance
Lightning Source LLC
Chambersburg PA
CBHW020816130626
46554CB00006B/2461